José "Pepe" Mujica
THE LABYRINTHS OF LIFE

Dialogue with Kintto Lucas

Tintají

Tintají, 2020
ISBN: 9798650321262

In Italy it was published with the title José "Pepe" Mujica I
LABERINTI DELLA VITA. Dialogue with Kintto Lucas.
Translation by Lucilla Soro. Castelvechi Editorial, 2018.

In Spanish it was edited by Ediciones Tintají, Quito, 2019.

To San Cono…

José "Pepe" Mujica
THE LABYRINTHS OF LIFE

What strength we had! What strength! We long for her of course and above all we long for not being able to transmit it to the new generations. We live it in a moment, in a spark of history, in today's world it is unthinkable. So much Don Quixote, so much poetry, is unthinkable ...

José "Pepe" Mujica

INTRODUCTION
by Kintto Lucas

1.

Punta Carretas

"The Homeland calls us, Orientals to the Front," was the slogan that presided over the first act of the Broad Front, back in March 1971. He had been under siege, social confrontation, and the actions of Tupamaro questioned traditional power with its corruption and fraud. . The repression of the right wing sectors, the military and paramilitary forces was increasing and the country was moving towards a dictatorship that would be consolidated in 1973.

It was in that 1971, in the Punta Carretas prison that I met José Pepe Mujica. At 8 years old, I was a regular visitor to that Montevideo prison. There, together with Pepe, my older brother, Enrique, was detained for belonging to the National Liberation Movement - Tupamaros.

The visits were on Saturdays and it was almost never absent. For me it was quite a rite: getting up at five in the morning, taking a bus, arriving long before the hour, stopping at the cafeteria located in front of the prison entrance, having a cappuccino with biscuits, which was one of the reasons why it was not missing.

Then go through the inspection booth, get to the place where the detainees were, chat, leave, go through the booth again, reach the street, walk towards the coast and feel that inexplicable feeling that the sea and its freedom produced in me, and then turn back to the mole with its closure.

Punta Carretas, was the high security prison reserved for tupamaros. In those days, most of the leaders were detained with Raúl Sendic at the helm. One of those imprisoned guerrillas was Pepe Mujica, whom he saw every Saturday during the visit, until the massive escape in September. In those days nobody could imagine that some decades later he would become President of Uruguay.

My brother had been arrested in June 1971. On Saturday, September 4, we took him to a pair of boots that he had ordered the previous week. Joy was common in visits, jokes, jokes ... That day, the atmosphere was more festive. In the farewell that "until next week and good weekend", they had a rare emphasis on prisoners. There was an optimism that was transmitted from the inside out. Something announced. At dawn on Monday 6, 106 guerrillas escaped, who crossed the street through a tunnel built for months.

Enrique, who had participated in the excavation and construction of the tunnel, along with Pepe Mujica and other tupamaros, finally did not escape. He changed cells the day before and left his place where he faced the tunnel. He did not have a complicated judicial process and it was managed that in a few months he could be exiled to Chile.

Pepe Mujica was one of the escaped. The visit on the Saturday before the escape was the last time I saw him in that brief period. It will be many years before I find him again, first as militants during the reconstruction of the MLN-T (National Liberation Movement – Tupamaros) in 1985 and then as colleagues in the *Mate Amargo* newspaper. The escape, called "El Abuso", was a severe blow to the government and the repressive forces. Two months to go before the national elections. Punta Carretas no longer offered security for the regime. For this reason, the works to put the Punta de Rieles Prison into operation were rushed.

Thus, weeks later, along with the few "tupas" considered more "dangerous" that remained, Enrique would be transferred to the new prison, which looked like the concentration camps he had seen in the films about World War II. He will be there until March 1972, when he will be deported to Chile, where he will join the Tupamara leadership abroad. Of the fugitives, many, including Pepe, will return to jail some time later and will be imprisoned for more than 12 years, others will be assassinated by the army on April 14, 1972 and some will go abroad.

Pepe was arrested again and became one of the nine hostages of the Uruguayan dictatorship. For years we tried to keep track of those nine tupamaros, who in groups of three were taken from barracks to barracks, remaining isolated for a long time, sometimes in tanks with water up to their waist, systematically tortured. Sentenced to death. The MLN-T was defeated, but if it took any action, the hostages would be executed. During his arrest Pepe was wounded with six bullets.

My brother Enrique took responsibility for propaganda in the leadership of the MLN-T in Santiago. Among other activities, he devoted himself to working on a plot film that would transcend worldwide showing the tupamaro process, directed by Costa Gavras and starring Yves Montand, entitled State of Siege.

Then came the trips to Cuba and the subsequent residence in Buenos Aires in 1973, where he formed the Revolutionary Coordination Board representing the MLN-T, together with Miguel Enríquez of the Movement of the Revolutionary Left (MIR) of Chile, the Army of National Liberation (ELN) of Bolivia and the People's Revolutionary Army (ERP) of Argentina. It was a guerrilla structure that unified revolutionary organizations in the Southern Cone. After multiple political activities, he will head the ELN in Bolivia, which was fighting against the dictatorship of Hugo Banzer. There he will die in September 1976, in a confrontation with the Bolivian army.

In 1980, I had to leave Uruguay and go live in Brazil. In that country, as in so many other countries in the world, solidarity work was carried out with Uruguayan political prisoners, particularly with the hostages, whom we knew lived in extreme conditions. The years of the dictatorship were almost endless. There were moments when it seemed difficult for us to fall. But the persistence of the Uruguayan people led first to defeat the military's constitutional project in 1980 and then to mass mobilizations and protests that put dictators in check until their negotiated withdrawal in 1985.

2.

The "Mateadas"

In March 1985, after the return to democracy, political prisoners, including those who were part of the historical leadership of the MLN-T, were affectionately called old men. The slow return of the exiles also began. Immediately the reconstruction of MLN began. Few believed that this would be possible, taking into account the different experiences lived by the thousands of militants in prison, exile and within the country.

However, little by little, walking from neighborhood to neighborhood, with mate in hand, they began to talk to people. This is how the "Mateadas" emerged, a kind of small acts in which some of those who were hostages talked with people.

I returned to Uruguay in mid-1985 and joined the MLN as a militant, in neighborhood work, the "Mateadas" and the Frente Amplio. At that time, despite the fact that we belonged to different areas, we often met Pepe in central activities, and one of the topics we always discussed was how to insert ourselves socially and politically in the interior of the country, where it was difficult to work. the left.

That same year Mate Amargo was founded, a biweekly Tupamaro newspaper open to the left and progressive sectors of traditional parties. In a short time it became the best-selling newspaper in Uruguay. In the fortnight Pepe was a columnist and I wrote articles on the social and economic reality of the neighborhoods of Montevideo and the interior of the country. For years I toured neighborhoods and apartments. This activity brought me closer to political and social work with the interior of the country, which we knew was key for one day the left to come to government.

At that time we often met Pepe at the headquarters of the newspaper or the MLN to talk about the reality of the interior. Although we also talked about political reality, the issue of the interior worried us both, as it did Raúl Sendic.

The interior of Uruguay until that moment was almost forgotten by most of the left. Pepe and I, like many others, following strategies developed by Sendic, we assume from our journalistic and political trenches to claim that area of the country and help position the left in a place taken by the right. We talked about forms, languages, strategies and symbols, necessary to conquer the hearts of Uruguayans "from outside".

The "Mateadas" were a tool for permanent accumulation, for bonding with people, for participation. They were a kind of crash course in political praxis for young people. The work in the neighborhoods and the interior consolidated that practice.

3.
The legacy of Raúl Sendic

In December 1987, at the Luis Franzini stadium in Montevideo, the first great Tupamaro event was held, after democracy was restored. It was also the first time Sendic would speak in public. Months before, he had traveled to Cuba to carry out a treatment on his mouth and face, since when he was arrested in 1972 he was wounded in the mouth and never had adequate treatment. Rather, systematic torture made it worse.

Despite the two-year build-up, there was some expectation for the act. People were arriving little by little, and something that seemed impossible in that Montevideo summer finally happened: 22,000 people filled the stadium.

In some way, due to the political and social response that was being given, we believed that many people would come, but not the most optimistic thought about filling the stadium. We all looked at each other a little surprised. The event was opened by Pepe, Eleuterio Fernández Huidobro followed and Raúl Sendic closed.

That day placed many of us in the social and political dimension of what could happen in the future. For some like me, who felt the political commitment to the popular sectors almost from childhood, it was a kind of break, of location in a reality with which we had to be consistent and responsible.

With my interest, since those years ago, to always look strategically, I remember that I told Raúl that this act marked the field for young people towards the future. Sendic with that tranquility that characterized him, and his wisdom told me: "maybe yes, but it will depend a lot on us and on you, the youngest. In any case, the important thing is that you always be you and never lose your rebellion, because it is easy to be a political bureaucrat, it is difficult to maintain rebellion in the face of injustice."

The slogan "Frente Grande: A response from the people", summarized a revolutionary political, social and economic proposal, which moved the floor to the Uruguayan left, which was just beginning to locate itself in a new democratic period with lags of military tutelage.

When Raúl Sendic was released from prison, his thinking bet on the formation of a Great Front that went beyond the Broad Front and included all the progressive social and political sectors of the country. When Sendic spoke of expanding the Front, he was referring to a social and political consolidation that did not give in to principles

There are three characters that marked the history of the Uruguayan 20th century: José Batlle y Ordóñez because he knew how to strengthen the State to achieve social policies and laws, industrialize the country to raise it up, and tell the Church to dedicate itself to saving souls if it is that he could do it; Aparicio Saravia, because he gave the warning note about the forgetfulness of the field with the Batllista project and Raúl Sendic for rescuing that Uruguay from the sugarcane growers, the rice farmers, the others, and showing the decline of the "Switzerland of America".

Buried alive during his years in prison, he knew how to write economics essays on cigarette sheets that few could have done under these conditions. Upon leaving prison, he devoted himself to researching and writing about economic issues that are now being discussed by economists.

The letters to her children were true sociological treatises. It is worth resorting to his articles written thirty years ago to see how he anticipated the banking crises that then occurred in various countries, as he put the problem of external debt at the center of the debate in his writings already from prison, as he analyzed before the migratory explosion that would occur years later and the irruption of urban youth violence as a consequence of impoverishment and the increase in drug trafficking, among other events, and how it looked at Latin America.

In addition to that, his political clarity and ethics make him the most significant figure on the Uruguayan left in the 20th century and one of the great revolutionary leaders of America in that century.

Sendic died on April 28, 1989, in a Paris hospital, at the age of 63, a victim of Charcot's disease caused by abuse during his fourteen years of inhuman prison. "Bebe" as we used to call him, was an incomparable leader, the ethical image of politics. Tens of thousands of people gathered to bid farewell to the great leader.

I had to write an article for *Mate Amargo* with interviews with social leaders, but I had a hard time doing it. In that maze of the MLN headquarters, I saw Pepe, dejected by the death of the comrade. I told him that I didn't really feel like writing.

Then he told me: *"Bebe" was above all a countryman, a guy who, like no one on the left, understood the forgetfulness of the interior of Uruguay. Talk to people who come from the field. You are not depressed by the sadness of the moment. Raúl left us a story, he left us a way of doing politics related to ethics. It is now up to you and the people of your generation to make their own story. You have to remember what you need to remember, but the best tribute to Raúl is that they build their history without copying anyone.*

Beyond those words and some other conversation we had later about Sendic, in *Mate Amargo* we had various anecdotes with Pepe, but there is a very special one due to the symbolic, which is worth remembering.

4.

Artigas' rag

It was September 1989, we were in a small fortnightly office. That day we had to leave our recurring theme to talk about an event that occurred twenty years before: the taking of the city of Pando by Tupamaros commandos, of which he was one of its protagonists.

With two other fellow journalists, we prepared a special on the subject. So we set up a collective conversation so that, along with other colleagues who participated in the taking, he would tell his memory of that guerrilla action carried out on October 8, 69 in tribute to Che, two years after his death.

A talk without myths, without false heroism, a talk about the life they had to live. Various anecdotes and small stories, crossed with the memory of those who died that day.

When telling him that some still remembered when he in the middle of the road took things out of his bag and started to put together a Star, he gave a mischievous little smile that characterizes him until today and said: there was a problem with weapons because it had been said that no one carried long weapons, however many colleagues appeared with rifles ... and smiled again.

His group had to take the city's telephone exchange and cut communications: the officials were reduced, taken to a room, then two guerrillas cut the cables on the roof. He laughed again, and explained that that was not enough. Then he added: we had to talk to the operators and ask them for collaboration.

Days later, old Pepe and the MLN leadership evaluated the takeover of the city: there we realized that although we had suffered a military defeat, it was a political victory. The prestige increased and many people began to approach the organization. The effect I cause.

There are even some anecdotes that illustrate this. For example, a boy who walked behind a companion without knowing that she was a "tupa", to become the fatal guerrilla, injured his arm and said he had done it in Pando. Instead of conquering her, he managed to stop her from giving him any more balls and he took off ... (he laughed out loud). But now at twenty years old I think that taking Pando should have been done much better ...

Suddenly Pepe cleared his throat and there was a silence, as of deep respect for the old man, who at that time was not so much but we all assumed that. Some eyes met with some complicity waiting for his words.

There, just while drinking a mate, with a low tone he sentenced us: that was the first time that the organization used a flag. When we were planning, seeing that we were going to take a police station, we realized that a banner was necessarily necessary. And we didn't have them! Because unlike that groups or parties, where everything is created before having the content, in the MLN things were not done that way. We were a revolutionary organization with years of fighting and we lacked a flag. Then it had to be created, necessity demanded it. We talked about it, and it didn't require much discussion. We solved it easily.

The idea was to use the "artiguista" flag (referring to José Gervasio Artigas)..

Artigas, rebellious and combatant, was born again at that time. There was his flag, on the mast of the Pando police station. One hundred and fifty years later, two generations merged into the struggle. After that flag has flown on many sides, it is no small matter. Now there is the rag ...

Neither when we had that conversation in Mate Amargo could anyone imagine that Pepe would become president, I think not even a legislator. That possibility did not seem to be in the minds of many colleagues.

5.

The Hugo Chávez rebellion

Until 1992 we were partners with Pepe in the MLN-T and in Mate Amargo. In May of that year I would go to live in Ecuador. But a few months before my trip, another event occurred that crossed our path. Just started February we were in the newsroom, closing the last pages, when suddenly the news of a military uprising in Venezuela emerged.

The information was confusing and speculation was swift. The right spoke of an attempted coup, a large part of the left compared the rebels with the Argentine "carapintadas" who had imposed their fascist gaze on the governments of Raúl Alfonsín and Carlos Menem, many did not understand what was happening and some decided to claim the right to doubt.

Although the newspaper was almost closed, we could not ignore the fact: we had to write about it and I accepted the challenge. Pepe smiled, because nobody wanted to "grab that pig" and without knowing what he was going to write, he supported me.

From the beginning I did not believe that it was an attempted coup d'etat like the ones we had suffered in the south of the continent. The language used also had no similarities to that of the "carapintadas", and the corrupt government of Carlos Andrés Pérez, which deepened the gap between rich and poor, did not inspire any confidence.

The best thing was to start with the language: first analyze the image of the events and their outcome, and then, above all, see what was hidden behind the words written and spoken in the proclamations of the rebels.

The analysis of the facts showed that it was not an attempted coup because the power rested with the high command, which emerged triumphant in the short term by repressing the rebels, defending the order established by the corruption surrounding Carlos Andrés Pérez.

As before, he had defended private property by blood and fire before the arrival of the desperate people who descended from the hills in the "Caracazo" (referring to the popular rebellion in Caracas in February 1989). If anyone could strike, it was precisely the high command.

But it was from studying the words that the most relevant data emerged. If I had looked at the rebels' discourse from a traditional leftist perspective, perhaps I would have been disappointed because they did not vindicate the working class, nor Marx, nor Cuba. They only claimed the ethics of fighting corruption and the image of Bolívar.

But that was not much if we take into account that the "carapintadas" also claimed the fight against corruption and the image of San Martín, and the Uruguayan dictatorship also claimed Artigas.

However, when analyzing each paragraph, the differences began to emerge between the fascist syntax discourse of the "carapintadas" and that of the Venezuelan officers who, although not clearly defined ideologically, demonstrated a link with the history of popular struggles.

When putting the pieces of the puzzle together, I found that discourse different from that of the Southern Cone military, I found a corrupt government supported by a worn out military dome, I found an economic model that consumed the wealth of oil among few, I found the "Caracazo" as an inorganic response to that model, and repression as an organic response to the despair of the people. I also found the ghost of a lost left in the discourse of social democracy.

At the time of writing, I started with language and opted to completely discard the image of coup, assuming that of a rebellion. I also chose to develop the analysis of the discourse and argue that the fact itself revealed a discontent with the political and economic leadership of a country devastated by poverty.

I also explained that the rebels were a purely Venezuelan product, emerged from Venezuela, without a foreign gaze. There were no "carapintadas", no coup plotters, no Peruvian-style or Peronist military. It was not a process that could be pigeonholed within traditional parameters.

However, the germ of a new perspective could be perceived, not as ideological as we were used to, but rooted in the defense of sovereignty, closely linked to a national and deeply popular reason for being. The basis of a different historical process that was taking place in Venezuela and in a sector of that country's armed forces.

When *Mate Amargo* was in the kiosks, many acquaintances of the Uruguayan left called me to say that he was giving a coup leader the place he did not deserve, they also defended Pérez and repudiated that rebellion.

Thus, like the mainstream media, they opted for the language of power. Both Jorge Zabalza, editor of the newspaper at the time, and Pepe and other colleagues agreed with my article. Years later, Pepe will establish a great friendship with Hugo Chávez, and I will have to work with both of them in the Latin American integration process.

<h1 style="text-align:center">6.</h1>

<h1 style="text-align:center">The link with Ecuador</h1>

After traveling to Ecuador, we did not lose communication, but we did lose the most frequent exchange. When I traveled to Montevideo, we sometimes talked about Uruguayan politics and the advance of the left, but a new topic will appear: the struggle of the Ecuadorian indigenous movement, which in Uruguay aroused curiosity.

Pepe, kept track of the struggles in Ecuador and my steps in the Andean country. Since my arrival in Quito, I was linked to the indigenous movement, participated in mobilizations and uprisings, either as a committed journalist or as a militant. In addition to the family bond, close work with social struggles tied me to a country where I thought I would only be a year, because I did not want to be away from Uruguay for a long time.

Interested in the processes of Latin America, every time I went to Uruguay I asked myself about organizational aspects, links with production, the land problem, the cultural issue, the forms of struggle. He identified with a movement he did not know. He knew that he and the indigenous people of Ecuador were part of the "others". Little by little, with Julio Marenales, one of the great leaders of the MLN, also hostage to the dictatorship, we helped build a link between some sectors of the Ecuadorian indigenous movement and the MLN.

7.

The "Pepe Phenomenon"

In the campaign for the presidential elections of October 2004, a controversy was generated about the popularity of Pepe Mujica. His growth in voting intention led leaders of traditional parties to carry out a dirty campaign of attacks, which was launched by former President Julio María Sanguinetti,

Months before, the leaders of the traditional parties refused to attack him because they believed, or were advised, that he was counterproductive, but that attitude did not stop his growth. On that occasion, after enduring several attacks, Pepe reacted. As soon as I saw that reaction, I wrote to him and the colleagues saying not to react because that was what his detractors wanted. I emphasized that the best way was to make fun.

Experienced on the one hand, and advised by their marketing advisers, those politicians wanted Pepe to get angry and respond to get into a confrontation and try to discredit him. At that time I wrote an article that had important repercussions, in which I spoke of the contempt of those sectors of the right, including some of the Frente Amplio, towards the "others", the different, such as Pepe.

The right, and even some sectors of the left, justified the electoral support for the former guerrilla, as part of a media phenomenon that they called 'Pepe Mujica Phenomenon'. Thus, they tried to empty their political actions and proposals of content.

Before the 'Pepe Mujica Phenomenon' at the media level, there was an action in accordance with certain principles, but above all with a fundamental one: the recovery of the interior as a human sector and geographical area that makes the country live, the recovery of man and the woman from the interior as a factor in the construction of an integrated country before the country's insertion in a globalized world, and the recovery of the interior as a very important factor in the construction of a productive country.

I wrote to Pepe from Ecuador, commenting on that vision about part of the Uruguayan left, always so Montevidean that he forgot about the interior. I said that it is difficult for him to get muddy because he is afraid of mud. That phrase caught his attention and he will remind me of it years later when he ran for president and I wrote about the emergence of the "others" in Latin American politics.

Pepe Mujica knew how to see the crucial question of 'interioran' forgetting, which is like saying forgetting the 'other', the 'different', which those who hegemonized the cultural construction left aside. In Ecuador, the irruption of indigenous peoples into the social and political life of the country meant the irruption of the 'other', of the different, who assumed their place in history.

The plural reality of the country was manifested when the indigenous emerged as an important actor in sociopolitical life. Then it was assumed that the 'other' exists and that it has its differences and its rights, and it must be respected to build a more integrated country. This manifestation has an ethnic image marked by the characteristics of Ecuador and the Andean world.

In Uruguay, where the indigenous people were exterminated by the founder of the Colorado party, the 'other' has an 'internal' image with all that it represents.

When José Mujica breaks into the Uruguayan Parliament, he is the 'other' who begins to take a place reserved almost exclusively for those who drank imported whiskey. It is the emergence of the 'other' in Uruguayan politics. But that 'other' has a particularity, in addition to his internal ancestry, he has an intellectual formation that allows him to move in any field and grow anywhere.

In the 2004 electoral campaign there was an irruption of the towns of the interior that began to stop consuming politics to go on to build it, it was the definitive irruption of the 'other' as the protagonist of Uruguayan sociopolitical life. The figure of José Mujica grew because he knew how to understand the 'other', and he understood it because he knew how to be part of it. Without over ideologizing, with theory and practice, and with a great deal of common sense.

Understanding that reality must be changed from daily life, because it is there that power relations begin to change, where a different imaginary begins to be built, which in turn helps to build a different society. Contempt for the 'other' is like contempt for clay. Although clay is still the best material to build.

Finally the Broad Front won the election for the first time. Tabaré Vázquez was the new president, Pepe was elected senator and his sector had a great vote. However, that campaign created fear in many citizens.

8.

Towards the presidency

In those days I did an interview with Pepe for a left-wing newspaper that I directed in Ecuador, called Tintají. We touch on some political issues. Regarding the National Liberation Movement - Tupamaros assured me that if it continued to exist it was for having maintained its dignity and its principles, and at the same time for having known how to be flexible, among other things because it was never a party but a movement. "For us flexibility, openness, were always a budget."

Then he added: "We do not err substantively in matters of the line, and this makes our interpretation of what national liberation means. This is an issue in which the left has fallen into different confusions, for example, thinking that national liberation is the same as socialism " And he exemplified: "Sweden is surely a country that has made its national liberation, which does not mean that it is going towards socialism."

For Mujica, achieving this intermediate goal enabled "to make honest alliances with vast sectors and have an open discourse, but maintaining the principles. Alliances and discourses that are socializing in some way but suffer the contradictions of a national liberation process. We must negotiate agreements, many agreements. "

Still, he admitted that national liberation represents only one stage. "It does not mean that the story is finished there, but for us it was always a determining and prerequisite. I am closer to Marx than to Lenin, because I do not believe that a poor society, intellectually subject and without high training can consider the construction from a higher society. If you want to, you can build a monster, as it has already happened. "

In December 2007, back in Uruguay, I met again with Pepe, who was Minister of Livestock. Returning to Uruguay always contained a discovery and a rediscovery, much more if it was a matter of spending almost a month in the country as it had not been for a long time, and at a time when an interesting political process was going on with the

Frente Amplio government, although with the own contradictions of processes carried out by wide movements in the politicians and multiculturalists in the social.

On that trip, it was the last time that I saw Mario Benedetti receiving a decoration from Venezuelan President Hugo Chávez in the beloved old Auditorium of the University of the Republic, a historical monument of the popular struggles of Uruguay and Latin America, where Che and so many joint voices of students and workers were forged.

Those days in Uruguay were enough to glimpse that Pepe Mujica had everything to be the future president of Uruguay. Pepe not only had the ability to dialogue, unify criteria and interpret the Uruguayan idiosyncrasy like few others. But it had also become the main gateway for people in the interior of the country who had previously fled from the left.

With more experience, a philosopher of life, a man of the country and the city, a genius of common sense, Mujica had managed to transcend the Front Wide frontier to become a national leader.

In those days we talked with Pepe about the interesting process that was opening in Ecuador after the election of Rafael Correa, who always contributed with his analyzes for Tintají, and with the installation of the Constituent Assembly. When talking about the Uruguayan reality, I told him that I had everything to be the next president.

Perhaps the distance, made me see a reality that many MLN-T colleagues did not see. Days later I wrote an article analyzing that possibility. Two years were left for the elections, with a more accentuated work of the militancy, the strengthening of an ethical image before the public opinion and a better communication with the young people assuming their language and their demands, in one year, it would become the best front-line option.

I had no doubt that Pepe Mujica was going to be the president, but many colleagues laughed. They told me: it is your heart, your father, that makes you see that, but it is impossible for him to become a candidate and then president. Don't put those ideas in the Old Man's mind. As my way of being makes me act according to what I think, I insisted on the option and worked to position it publicly. Pepe took it humbly, but did not discard the proposal.

On my return to Ecuador, in January 2008, I went as an advisor to the Constituent Assembly's Sovereignty, Integration and International Relations Commission, where I will be until its promulgation of the new Constitution in July. Then I intensely militated in the campaign for its approval in a Plebiscite in September of that year.

In March 2009, during an interview for a network of radio stations in Ecuador, when asked a question by me, Correa said that the election of Pepe Mujica as President of Uruguay in October of that year would be a sign of the deepening of the changes in that country. "An eventual election of José Mujica, would mean a deepening of the changes that are taking place in Latin America and more specifically in South America and Uruguay," said the Ecuadorian president, highlighting that the changes began with Tabaré Vázquez.

Correa made a parallel between the meaning that Pepe's election would have and the one that the arrival of Nelson Mandela to the government had at the time for South Africa, and said that he would be the Uruguayan Mandela. The Ecuadorian president highlighted the processes of change in South America, with governments that are making the largest social investment in decades, because they have a clear option for the poor.

At that time, according to pre-election polls in Ecuador, Rafael Correa would be reelected in the first round of the presidential elections scheduled for April 26, with the rules of the new Constitution. While in Uruguay the polls indicated that José Mujica would win the primary elections of the government leader Frente Amplio in June, and in October he could be elected President of the country.

Both Rafael Correa and José Mujica showed a clear interest in strengthening the integration of Latin America. "The key to rebuilding Latin American society is to break neoliberalism and replace it with a coexistence based on cooperation and social solidarity," said Correa. For his part, during the launch of his campaign in Montevideo, Mujica praised the government of Rafael Correa and other leftist presidents in South America.

"The fate of those who live matters, how they live, that's why thanks to the Tabaré (Vázquez), the Lula (Da Silva), the Evo (Morales), the (Rafael) Correa, those who fight as they can and darn. They are opening a different horizon that we could not even imagine 30 years ago, "said José Mujica

"Governing with a progressive vision is darning every day, permanently forming alliances, trying to widen the support base as much as possible, trying to iron out the most dangerous contradictions, worrying about wages, worrying day by day about work, worrying because the thick slice does not condemn others to starvation ", assured the tupamaro leader at that time.

At that time I felt comforted to contribute in the approach between Pepe and Correa, and between the Uruguayan and Ecuadorian left.

<h1 style="text-align:center">9.</h1>

<h2 style="text-align:center">As is ...</h2>

Days later, I wrote an article entitled "Pepe as is ..." that analyzed Mujica's authenticity.

Juan Carlos Onetti once said: "The most important thing I have about my books is a feeling of sincerity. Of having always been Onetti. Of never having used any trick ... of never having cheated myself or anyone else. All the weaknesses that can be found in my books are my weaknesses and are real weaknesses. " I think it was in an interview with María Esther Gilio. If someone read Onetti's work and read his life, there is no doubt that it was so. His work is a reflection of his life and his life is a reflection of his work. It would never have occurred to him to make Santa María a soap opera town, for example.

There is no doubt that when you listen to José Mujica speak you notice a feeling of sincerity and immediately perceive that Mujica has always been Mujica, that he has not used any trick ... that he has not cheated on himself or anyone, and that all the strengths and weaknesses that can be found in his speech and in his actions are his strengths and weaknesses.

When people vote for Mujica they know they are voting for someone who never cheated on himself or cheated on anyone. And if we analyze that authenticity a little bit, perhaps we will find it at the bottom of something that some call it Uruguayan. That strange thing that sometimes we do not know what it is, but we know that it exists when the drums sound, or a "murga" appears on stage, or we see some children playing soccer in the street, or we enter the University Auditorium or the Hall of the Lost Steps ...

On those days I went to work in the Coordinating Ministry of Politics of the Correa government, where I created the Political Strategy Council. I spent months there, but in June I went to Montevideo for a week to participate in the internal election of the Frente Amplio. In October, before the presidential election, I left the government of

Ecuador and went to participate in Pepe's electoral campaign. I couldn't stop participating.

Pepe won the elections in the second round against Luis Alberto Lacalle and the Frente Amplio had a parliamentary majority. At the end of November, after the second round, I wrote an open letter to Pepe entitled "Notes for a Letter to a Fellow President" that said:

> Dear Companion José Mujica, Old Pepe:
>
> There are mixed feelings and feelings in these hours. I think of the giant flag of Otorgués that arrives in Ejido at the old Ramírez beach from so many encounters and disagreements in my world as a guru. Hundreds, thousands of flags. The moon rises and the breeze brings a fresh air like that brought by young people to this electoral campaign. Young people have taught a lesson, so often learned and unlearned: you cannot go back or forth from the town, you have to walk alongside them.
>
> Seeing Galeano conversing with you the night before the election, in a place full of people from various countries in the Americas below, and feeling that they are there is like claiming Uruguay. Eduardo is part of the best image in the country. More than any Minister or ambassador, part of Uruguay respected and admired abroad.

See the town this Sunday in the streets, a town that feels like part of you. See several companions and companions who could be to live it with bright eyes. How many tears of emotion came from our eyes, our hearts and our memories this Sunday!

Never better to remark, as you did that this battle was given by so many anonymous companions who did not appear for the photo at the time of the victory, and that they had to be on the stand. Back in January, when so many doubted that you could be a candidate, I wrote in an article, resorting to Hegel, that you gathered around you various symbolic elements that placed you as a part inextricably linked to the spirit of the time. The spirit of the time is built by the peoples.

There are times when people take a step back and let the rushing run. So those in a hurry think they are going fast, looking for shortcuts, and they resemble a runaway horse. Finally the least hurried, who came behind, arrive next to the towns.

There are times when people get tired of waiting for those who are too late, for those who believe that the road is part of the bureaucracy. Then they go over them and they run wild, they rebel, they stop believing. Those who are always left behind, see that people leave, walk away and can run wild. Then the right wins. There they wonder what to do without people and curse people ...

There is a time to initiate changes and another to deepen them. The deepening of these changes must be done at the right time, neither before nor after. The moment when people accompany building their future, creating and recreating the individual and collective dream. You have to know that people can accompany you but it does not mean that they go with you to build reality.

You have to know how to understand when people go with you helping to create and recreate that individual and collective dream, of which a government can only be a small part, and when it only accompanies you without getting involved in the journey.

What would this campaign have been without those young people who called to defend joy. Without the people who gambled despite those who believe that the road is a well-squared box, quiet, institutionalized, almost as much as the central premises of the Frente Amplio. What would have become of the people if you had not revived hope. What would have become of you without people and without hope.

The Companion choice, Old Pepe, puts you in a huge compromise. No one has such a great commitment to people like you, and you almost-almost have no right to fail. No President has had such a large commitment. It is hard, but it is so companion.

It is so for all your history, that of all moments. This is the case for all those who are not here and who played to make this country and America below something better, some leaving their lives very young, as young as those who turned the campaign around today. This is because Latin America has a great hope in you. This is because Orientals and Orientals see that you are almost a photograph of hope.

Companion, a government is built with passion, with reason and with efficiency. But no progressive government is built without people. This time is a time to dream, to reinforce hope, to build utopias, tomorrow will be a time for dreams, hopes and utopias to tie with reality. Never forget that you pass, but people follow, tied to a story written by those who survive, tied to a possible hope, tied to their dreams of the future.

Old Pepe, don't let hope get lost. What a little Taraite it is. But that's life. Surely you will face it as you always faced it, seeking and looking for this little country to be a little better, a little more equal, a little more of all and of all.

In these hours, remembering my brother Enrique, who fell thinking-making the revolution; I also think about that enormous challenge of ensuring that young people do not get in the way. Staying on the road is no longer finding death in a confrontation, it is getting tired of the stones laid by old and young bureaucrats.

Staying on the Camino can be leaving the country to be a foreigner everywhere, including the country because you did not have the necessary place to continue on the path. Staying on the road is not just the lack of a job, it is the lack of a space for participation where to comment and decide, where to help build the road, without being used ...

Now, always remembering Raúl Sendic, the young and the old Raúl. The one from whom we learned so much, and from whom we continue learning. The Raúl of the sugar cane marches and the economic analyzes shedding light. The Raúl of dignity, staying in the country when he could have left as you once said. El Raúl and who bet on young people, on the true commitment and creativity of young people. Now, remembering your own way, dear friend, Old Pepe, now is a good time to tell you as always, that there will be a homeland for everyone, surely there will be a homeland for everyone ...

10.

An endless path

I returned to Ecuador with the joy of having lived to tell this new story, and in part to have been the protagonist. In January 2010, I go as an advisor to the Ministry of Foreign Affairs of Ecuador and in May I am appointed Vice Minister, where I will spend two years with intense work in the consolidation of a new foreign policy and Latin American integration. On many issues we work together with Pepe, such as the ratification of the Unasur (Union of South American Nations) Convention and its strengthening. Two by three we met at international meetings.

On September 30, 2010, there was an attempted coup against the Rafael Correa government in Ecuador, and the kidnapping of the president himself. Given the situation, we divided tasks with the Chancellor: he devoted himself to internal political work and I to international work.

The first person I called to start the campaign of international denunciation of the coup was Pepe Mujica, who immediately contacted the President of Argentina, Cristina Fernández, and other presidents to convene an urgent meeting of South American leaders. That day, at all times Pepe was concerned, consulting me as the events unfolded until Correa was released.

In April 2012 I resigned from my position as Vice Chancellor for disagreeing with the signing of the Ecuador Free Trade Agreement with the European Union, but we remain friends with Rafael Correa.

In June 2012, I traveled to Montevideo to present the book As is - José Mujica's path to the presidency-, which brings together chronicles of the 2009 campaign. Pepe was present and spoke on the spot.

At the end of 2012, Pepe proposed that I return to Uruguay to be the government's Secretary of Communication. The news leaked before the appointment, and the right-wing media campaigned with articles and editorials saying that my appointment would be a danger to freedom of expression.

After twenty years out of the country I was treated as an intruder. In the face of that campaign, the appointment was discarded. Months later, Pepe appointed me Itinerant Ambassador for Unasur, Celac (Community of Latin American States) and Alba (Bolivarian Alliance for the Peoples of Our America) with the aim of linking Uruguay more with these integration processes.

There were months of contradictions with the Vice President who sought to bring the neoliberal Pacific Alliance closer to the country and, above all, with the Uruguayan Foreign Minister Luis Almagro, who worked closely with the United States embassy and acted according to the guidelines of the ambassador herself.

Their attitudes against integration and the progressive project became increasingly evident. In response, I informed Pepe and then resigned with a letter in which I made clear Almagro's actions. Years later, in a meeting with Pepe, he acknowledged his mistake for trusting him and pointed out the enormous disappointment for the betrayal path at the beginning of the former Uruguayan foreign minister, who from the OAS assumed a position contrasted with that of Pepe and Latin America.

They have been years of friendship and joint work with Pepe Mujica, from various instances. Life placed us in important moments in the political construction of Latin America, but the road never ends ...

THE LABYRINTHS OF LIFE

In the 1960s and early 1970s, a guerrilla
organization in Uruguay achieved international
sympathy, for its political-military actions, the
National Liberation Movement - Tupamaros
(MLN-T), which assumed the symbols of the
independentista revolutionary José Artigas . In that
movement, people from various left organizations
came together, one of the leaders was José Pepe
Mujica, who many years later would become
president of that country.

This conversation is a contribution to reflection on
the reality of today's world. Global politics and
economy, progressive governments and social
struggles, the peace agreement in Colombia, the
difficulties of Venezuela and the legacy of Hugo
Chávez, the parliamentary coup in Brazil, current
capitalism and the culture of consumerism, the
meaning of democracy, the need to consolidate the
integrating process, the international policy of the
United States, the future of the peasants and the
control of seeds by the transnational corporations,
socialism and the quixotes who were left on the
road, are some of the topics covered in this two-
voice dialogue.

KINTTO LUCAS. Talking with Pepe is like walking through memories and entering the labyrinths of life, but it is also analyzing the present with a future projection. This is a talk between two colleagues who share some moments of common political militancy, that we have had agreements and disagreements, but above all that we continue to share Tupamara roots.

Old Pepe today is a reference in different countries, especially for many young people. There are many issues to deal with, but perhaps we should start with the peace agreement in Colombia. Yesterday the peasants looked at the war as part of a road.

Today they remember so many struggles that they lived and so many that they did not live, because there are already so many years, that there are several generations. They went back from the war and now they remember the past, almost, almost reaching peace. Some still wonder what is peace? Is peace worth it? In Colombia people see peace as part of a road that is being built. A difficult fabric because sometimes the threads do not match on the loom. But you have to find a match ...

JOSÉ MUJICA: I think that, although it was a negotiation that took four years, precisely, that time that was endless for many, is showing the effort and the seriousness of the effort, the commitment behind it. It is not anything that was agreed. On the one hand, it has as a gigantic thing the promise of ending a long conflict, obvious, whose social, political and economic dimensions are very difficult to measure.

Over there, from the point of view of the economy, there are those who make calculations that could be more or less four times the Marshall Plan, to give an idea ... But in reality, analyzing the set of things surrounding the agreement to make it possible We see that it is a country project for a new Colombia.

Speaking of the peasant theme that you mention: his chapter dedicated to the Earth, for example, is transcendent. Colombia is a country where probably 60% of the land has no title, no one knows who it was or anything and everything is in question, without a cadastre or institutionality, with twelve million poor peasants, who have been dedicated to production of coca.

They are economic populations marked by coca, which is sold for cash and sells well. The corn and beans that they can harvest are not enough to live on, there is an economic problem that determines the reality of the Colombian countryside. Sometimes we forget elementary things, but coca has been a form of subsistence for the poor in the middle of abandoned fields, forests, a geography without roads, without institutionality, without minimal social market organization, as to solve the trouble.

In this context, you have to understand the coca economy, which must also spill goods over the formal economy, because if you can't explain why Colombia has a GDP (Gross Domestic Product) like Argentina's, where does this come from, right? ? Magic? No, there is something that is not seen or measured.

Well, but the text of the agreement considers all that, because they know that this will be a real problem for the governments that are coming and for the FARC itself (the Revolutionary Armed Forces of Colombia) who are betting on convincing integrated politics.

Timochenko says: "Our weapon will be the word", and he wants to symbolize a lot with that. Of course there is a chapter of uncertainty, there is the story of what happened to the Patriotic Union with 5000 leaders assassinated. It is the history of

Colombia, which did not start yesterday, a country that has the tragic history of resolving its political conflicts with bullets. This agreement is also a lesson for all: the value of tolerance and coexistence in a society, because societies without contradictions, is nothing more than a pipe dream of the human race. Societies without contradictions do not exist.

KINTTO LUCAS. In Latin America and particularly South America, for some years we have been experiencing progressive government processes, as part of the post-neoliberal stage. However, as much as some have spoken of revolution or socialism and add a surname to them, the truth is that there was neither an attempt at revolution nor an attempt at socialism. And it seems obvious that it is impossible to reach socialism without first walking the path of national liberation.

Along this path, and as part of that process, it is necessary to appropriate democracy and resignify it. In Latin America in general and Ecuador in particular, democracy and political participation were reduced to the act of voting. However, democracy supposes the effective involvement of society in decision making. The democracy that we must achieve must be based on permanent debate and, above all, on a process where citizens are the managers of its development.

This radical democracy then supposes the construction of citizenship, that is to say, subjects of rights that can exercise power. Therefore, strengthening democracy implies promoting social participation in all its forms. This radical democracy must be brought to all areas of social life: to the State, to companies, to the neighborhood, to the political movement, even to the family.

In the Ecuadorian case, although formally the rights of citizenship were extended to the population as a whole, in practice we had second-class citizens, relegated due to their economic condition or ethnicity. In this sense, citizenship must be extended to the entire population, which does not imply, of course, a process of cultural homogenization that threatens the particularities of peoples and nationalities. So, the process of national liberation towards socialism goes through the construction of a citizen democracy, which also means recovering collective action from the neighborhoods and communities, and recovering social mobilization.

JOSÉ MUJICA. Okay, but human beings, apart from class differences, which are notorious, we have differences that are of individuals, even within classes. Nature makes us similar, but with a particular hairline, it does not do identical and equal things like the one that makes bricks, no. Therefore we must think that due to our imperfections, conflicts in societies are inevitable. So, the capital of tolerance to coexist is not, as we could think at one time, a liberal by-product of the bourgeoisie, in reality it is a value for the human race, against which it is not necessary to back down, on the contrary it must be defended .

Those of us who have always been a bit challenged, fighting and with everything else, we have to realize that it is a value to defend. I would almost say that it is the most essential thing that the idea of Democracy can have. How can we coexist in Democracy if we do not support the differences that exist in coexistence?

One over the years begins to discover some things. For example, I believe that social classes have history, and because they are subject to history, they have notable differences in their different stages. The feudal lords of the 8th and 9th century, who lived in stone castles that looked like barracks, are not the same, sometimes eaten by bedbugs and lice, warlords, dressed in armor; that the feudal lords of the XV and XVI century who leave the armor and put on a loop, with refined hands and gestures, who become courtiers of the kings. They are not the same, they are feudalisms but very different.

In this sense, the founding, Quaker bourgeoisie, which makes work and savings mythic as national pride, is not the same; than the cumulative and speculative bourgeoisie of our contemporary financial system.

They are not the same, there is a difference even though they belong to the same class, right? So, analyzing these things, we also see that it is necessary to take care of the factor of coexistence, which is the greatest challenge facing Colombia.

KINTTO LUCAS. Colombia and Uruguay are quite different countries. The guerrillas were also different, even due to the geography of each country. However, the fact that the MLN –T, after its military defeat, of so many prisoners, dead, disappeared, was inserted into legal policy, and even you became president, perhaps it is an example to take into account by the FARC, or maybe not? ...

JOSÉ MUJICA. I think so. Humbly, in what is particular to me, I have talked at length two or three times with the FARC leadership that was in Havana about these things. In the battery of arguments towards vacillations, the opposition, the people who think No, say that the agreements hand over power to the FARC: "Tomorrow they will be in power, because they have this, because they have the other," they say.

That's a fantasy, reasoning like that is a fantasy. In this sense, it is like thinking that we came to government because of our guerrilla history. It is not like this! People don't vote guerrillas, because people look back a little, but a little, not much, sometimes too little I would say, because we have our eyes forward.

People hope to know how it goes at the fair tomorrow. She is worried if she has a job or if they solve her financial problems, if she has to pay for electricity, and all that. Now we even know a little more than we did before. We know that when people are able to overcome chronic poverty, they insert themselves into the consumer society and want more.

Then it becomes more demanding, and becomes critical. What you attended to yesterday believing that it was a fantastic progress, basically you only helped him insert himself into the consumer society (chuckling). There you have to feel the honeys of what happens to the PT in Brazil !, for example. True?

Don't expect gigantic gratitude from the masses because they left poverty, just like that, if you couldn't develop a degree of consciousness. If people realized that this improvement did not come about by spontaneous generation or personal merit, but by the political struggle of human beings, perhaps they would understand better and be more involved in the processes.

So there are no thanks or acknowledgments (between laughs). We didn't know that, now we feel it ... and we have to learn. Surely people have the right to continue improving, but I have my doubts about what it means to improve more ...

KINTTO LUCAS. (Laughing) Sure, and what is to improve as well?

JOSÉ MUJICA. Yes, what is improving as well? Because there it is, capitalism has sown an idea of permanent progress that is linked to economic improvement to consume more things, so improving means consuming more. He also invented things to be short-lived (laughs), right? Then the idea was created that progress never ends. There the other question arises: in this progress, is man happier?

There the thing changes. What there has been from investigations in the field, as far as we know, if people are 20 or 30 years old they tend to believe that if they have more things they are happier, or if they have more power, more fame or more money, they are happier. But when he starts to pass 50, the guys start to think differently, right?

KINTTO LUCAS. It seems that progressive governments instead of creating citizens created consumers. But that is also in the model. They came out of neoliberalism, but they consolidated a consumption model that came from neoliberalism. There was a lot of talk about solidarity economy, but in a consumerist model it is impossible to strengthen a solidarity economy process.

And when the crisis appears, it seems that the easiest thing to do is to resort to adjustment. Radical democracy and the solidarity economy are part of the same process of national liberation and, obviously, of the same symbolic construction.

Consumer associations, cooperatives, agroecological production systems, worker-managed companies, which have been very important to you, the construction of houses for mutual aid and various economic organizations of this type, are often not recognized as such but as social instances of solidarity. So it is not assumed that they could stop being isolated if they are part of an economic model based on the solidarity economy, in which the State plays a cohesion role. An economic model that is not based on a solidarity economy does not achieve a better redistribution of wealth, therefore it does not eliminate the old gap between rich and poor, and it keeps intact the economic structures that caused the reality that is supposedly trying to change. The solidarity economy does not mean incorporating notions of solidarity in economic practices, it means transforming the economy.

The neoliberal sectors managed to install in the collective imagination that solidarity is necessary to solve certain social problems that the economy cannot overcome. Thus, solidarity is not part of the economy, it is only an action that appears after the economy has produced its effects. So "solidarity" is synonymous with charity or charity and ends up transforming is an element used so that everything remains the same.

The solidarity economy implies that solidarity is introduced into the economy itself, and that it operates and acts in the various phases of the economic cycle, that is, in production, circulation, consumption and, although it sounds contradictory, in accumulation. It proposes to transform the economy from within and structurally, generating a new economic rationality. It implies a model of solidarity development.

But it is not the same that solidarity is part of all instances of the economy, of companies, of the market, of the State, of consumption, of collective and individual spending, that there are certain solidarity behaviors within economic activities. Today, more than ever, we should consolidate the solidarity economy as an alternative, from outside and from within the State. But now some progressive governments are in decline.

In progressive governments, many people came out of poverty, they worked in the social sphere in different ways, but they were not able to change structures and, now, beyond the conservative advance, they are beginning to see a setback within the policies of those governments. How can the rise and decline of progressive governments be interpreted?

JOSÉ MUJICA. Surely there must be, as in any profound phenomenon, multiple causes, but I think that some fundamental ones are in the exhaustion of the possibilities that the system itself gives and not having been able to overcome the contradictions of the system itself.

And something very important, not having established a battle in the field of culture, a battle that replaces the culture of consumption.

At one time we thought that by changing the relations of production and distribution society changed mathematically, a serious mistake, we know that culture plays a determining role, more and more, and we do not participate in facing this cultural battle. The leaders suffered the same: we used the same cars, the same secretaries, the same rugs, the same paraphernalia, we sat at the same table where they sat, etc.

And at the end of so much negotiating and having to adjust the body, I think we are transferring confusion to people. In the image of the collective we are the same, although we are not, it does not matter, it is what we represent to people. I think in part, there may be some of that.

KINTTO LUCAS. Another fundamental issue, although it is sometimes used only as an excuse for not delving into economic changes, is the reality of today's world. The effect of the transnational economy, how inequality is accentuated, the increase in the concentration of wealth and the lack of responses to the middle classes in developed countries, new forms of exploitation, new human weaknesses and much more …

JOSÉ MUJICA. There is a historical pendulum to the right that is outside Latin America, it is in the world, because when you see the speeches in the United States and Europe ... I am not impressed by the ultra-right speeches, what impresses me is the people who follow those speeches, that they are not Martians, they are part of American and European society, world powers ... When I listen to those who vote against Merkel as if Merkel was an epicenter of the world revolution, I am concerned. Please! Has something come out to think that Merkel is a revolutionary? We are in a difficult moment of the world situation and that also influences Latin America.

This, in my opinion, is an unintended consequence of the effect of the rise of globalization with the rise of the transnational economy, which is producing, among other things, a concentration of wealth of a dreadful nature, accentuating inequality. It is not that it multiplies poverty, it multiplies the distance between rich and poor, inequality.

Huge sectors of the labor class, such as the American metal workers, are earning in value terms the same as they were in the year 79, while the GDP grew enormously. Where's that growth? Ah! He concentrated on a bunch of very few types, and the poorest types begin to perceive what is happening in their selves.

In other words, this world of the transnational economy comes hand in hand with a multiplication of the concentration of wealth, and it is not responding to huge sectors of the elementary middle class in developed countries, which also fills them with uncertainty.

For example, after NAFTA (North American Free Trade Agreement) the American auto industry left Detroit and other places and settled on the border with Mexico. One could say: this is good for Mexican workers who have jobs. But the guys earn a pittance and thousands also left the field because they can't compete with North American corn and wheat, and went to survive in the American industry based on the border. But still not everyone gets a job. Mexico lost two million peasants after NAFTA. But in turn, the wages of American metalworkers were frozen, because they cannot compete with the wages of Mexican workers. So who won in that story? Big companies won and production costs fell.

KINTTO LUCAS. There are the consequences of Mexico's Free Trade Agreement with the United States and Canada. Mexico no longer produces corn. But Colombia is also seeing how the field is liquidated with its FTAs with the United States and Europe. Other countries seem to want to go down the same path.

JOSÉ MUJICA. Sure, now Mexico, where the corn originated, has to import it from the United States. How about? Well then this produces a scam feeling. This kind of thing generates hyper-nationalism: the United States for the Americans, France for the French, Germany for the Germans ...

And the fault lies with the Chinese, those who come from outside, those who take away my work, those simplistic explanations that work election in people who have anguish and are hooked on speeches like Trump's about building the walls with Mexico and everything else. It is awful, because we saw that movie in the 1930s, but as the human being is the only bug capable of stumbling over the same stone many times, there is a boom in the "rights of the rights." We have to see the nuances, right?

KINTTO LUCAS. (Laughter) We also have to see our rights. There are some differences between those rights and ours ...

JOSÉ MUJICA. Sure, we have a right with which we can fight, we go to the smacks, but, more or less, it works within the framework. Now, another right arises that is against this right, speaks of race and has popular support.

We have experiences and antecedents on that, because Hitler came up with the votes, also Mussolini. The mass supported them. In this framework, we must see the history of what is happening in Latin America, because it is not as independent as it seems, and of course, our own mistakes, which are sometimes difficult to recognize.

KINTTO LUCAS. We from Ecuador, and in particular me as vice chancellor, were against NATO intervention in Libya because it would provoke a civil war of unpredictable consequences and would open the intervention in Syria. Then against the intervention in Syria, We said that what is happening today was going to happen.

That terrible civil wars were going to be generated with results of death, destruction and thousands of refugees. We said it and we repeated it a thousand times. The media attacked us and said that we were defenders of the Libyan and Syrian regime, that we would be isolated, and a whole lot more. Reality proved us right. That is of no use because the dead continue to flood the Mediterranean.

But now neither the big international media, nor those of our countries, that the only thing they know how to do is follow-upism, nor the politicians of the right, nor those of the left who did not have the capacity to see what would happen or preferred to accommodate, nobody says Nothing, they only disguise a face of supposed horror and show their hypocrisy. They made political use of human rights and devastated Libya to exploit it better. Now they destroy Syria.

Why is the Security Council not asking for an intervention in Guantánamo to verify the violation of human rights? It seems that the world is still a sham. NATO killed more people than Qaddafi and nobody says that. NATO countries kept Libya's money, not Gaddafi's, and nobody says that. Interventions bring more death to the countries in which it is intervened. There is a double standard in the world and that is reflected in international organizations. Controlling Syria is definitively controlling the Middle East.

When human rights violations are committed by the United States, or NATO, there are no convictions, nobody says anything. And we can transfer that to Latin America, for example in the case of Venezuela. Here, no young man from the OAS paid by the United States dollars comes out to say anything against the United States, but they run to run errands for him. There is a political use with Syria, as there was before in Libya. And there is a political use against Venezuela. While Gaddafi was a friend of those who later attacked him, there was no problem, he was not a human rights violator, but when he stopped being a friend, yes. Drug trafficking, terrorism, the fight against the guerrillas at certain times was also a political weapon of the great powers.

You have pointed out some mistakes that Venezuela has made, we could point out different mistakes, but who has not made mistakes. Beyond highlighting those errors that Venezuela has had: is there a right to intervene from outside? Can it be accepted that there are countries that want to intervene in Venezuela? Can you accept that some, who said they were from the left, openly work for the United States and serve as spokesmen for the intervention?

JOSÉ MUJICA. They have no right! No one has the right to intervene. But this is also sarcastic, very sarcastic, because Venezuela's errors and motives are theirs, and they have to solve them. They are not going to solve them from the outside, intervening. By intervening from outside they will create a situation of chaos, of civil war. Besides, what the fuck with democracy in Venezuela and they don't say a word about what happens in China!

KINTTO LUCAS. Or in Saudi Arabia.

JOSÉ MUJICA. Or in Saudi Arabia ... They don't say anything, do they? But there are plenty of examples to point to Venezuela, small warts next to the disasters that have occurred in the world. There they say nothing, because it is powers that influence the decisions of today's world that commit these disasters. So I cannot consider the tolerance of the United States with some countries that are its friends.

It is a fairly cynical policy to use human rights. Don't screw me! Human rights? If we look in recent years, the United States and its allies have a dire balance. Where they intervened there is nothing but disaster, disarticulation: Afghanistan, Iraq, Libya, Syria ... Look what they did! I bet the model they have for peace in Syria is balkanization, do what they did in Yugoslavia, balkanize it, take advantage of a Shiite Syria, another Sunni, Kurdistan and then atomized use them one by one ... God forgive me, but that movie too We have seen it many times ...

KINTTO LUCAS. Now, in this current, real Latin America that we are living, how can the reality of Brazil or Venezuela be interpreted? These are difficult times.

JOSÉ MUJICA. They are very difficult moments. At the signing of the Peace Agreement in Colombia, I was talking to Serra, the Brazilian

Chancellor, he grabs me and says: "Look, I know we are on the opposite side-he knows that I am a friend of Lula-but he reminded me that he was sheltered in Uruguay in the house of old Cultelli. Fall on your back! In old Cultelli's house! (1)

KINTTO LUCAS. This is life!

JOSÉ MUJICA. But you saw, that's life! You can't believe it, I didn't know, I didn't remember, if I ever knew. That right-wing chancellor who participated in the fall of Dilma, who was a candidate in some electoral campaign, was exiled in Uruguay, in the house of old Cultelli. And as much as we are on different sides, I'm not going to stop talking to him. It would be silly because the worst thing is to deny reality, but you know very well that I am a friend of Lula and what I think ...

There is one of the problems, the Venezuelan comrades do not know how to do politics, they have Cain's disease, statements are sent that are useless, because sometimes you have to make statements, but you have to see what results they give. We should not confuse noise with propaganda, said the Baby (Raúl Sendic).

One thing is the journalistic pact and the repercussion, another thing is what these statements leave you, because we need a policy of alliances and we cannot spit out what is closer or more hesitant, even if they are not ours, because doing that is a nice way to get more and more isolated. It does not seem to me that it is intelligent, it is possible that their internal policy is at the table, that is another story, but the foreign policy cannot be at the table, it should not be at the table.

But well, I am very concerned about Venezuela for several things, but there is also everything that Chavez sowed, everything, the most colossal fighter for Latin American Integration, without a doubt. The most generous government I have known in political history in the years when I can measure the history of Latin America.

Venezuela has been hit by this oil crisis enormously, in addition to a lack of political office, I believe that in Venezuela a set of reforms was needed a long time ago, particularly those that allow for a rational currency price and exchange rate, not crazy, because that destabilizes any economy and naturally pay the price. But the oil rent threw the peasantry to the coast and they ran out of peasants, so in Venezuela there is no culture of food production. Of course, that is no longer the responsibility of now, it is the son of history.

It is very different from Colombia, which has twelve million peasants. I never tire of saying that it is more difficult to train a peasant than an engineer. Because the peasant has a heritage of birth origin, belongs to a culture, he may be technically backward and have few means, but he has a capacity for symbiosis with his environment that is noticeable. So countries cannot neglect their peasants, and to remove them from technological stagnation and project them, they must rely on them as a creative force, they cannot leave them aside. France, which has a protectionist policy and has the peasants as in a garden, has cared for them, subsidizes them, has them as a model and you walk the French countryside and it seems a garden.

KINTTO LUCAS. And the German also …

JOSÉ MUJICA. And the German one too, right!

KINTTO LUCAS. But returning to the issue of refugees now arriving in Europe in the tens of thousands, and many are left on the road, in the Mediterranean, on the beaches, dead, dozens of children ...

JOSÉ MUJICA. It is a great paradox Europe that sent migrants around the world now wants to kick out those who arrive. And they come because of the war that the West sowed in Libya and Syria. But also Capitalism sowed the dream of the consumer stained glass window, and these emigrants of now are not the same as before. They are not like the immigrants we know, the old Italians and Galicians who came to our countries with the cardboard suitcase.

Today's emigrants have the internet, they have the telephone, they are connected to those who stay, and they don't even want to stay in southern Spain or Italy, they want to cut for Germany, for the industrial and wealthy north.

Of course, they are attracted by that cultural focus, by that image. Curiously, the subdued also have ages, they have histories ... The poor of today are not the same as the poor of fifty or a hundred years ago, these are more modern, therefore they are less primitive and weaker.

I think something similar happens to the law of zootechnics. When you cross beings very far from each other, in general they have some remarkable characteristics, they are usually more productive. And when you accentuate selection work, seeking to increase productivity, managing the laws of inheritance and characters, you are successful. For example, meat animals can have more loins, shorter legs, in short, you transform them in a long process.

But do not get excited, when you put something else on, it is taking other things from it and what is being taken from it ?: rusticity. That more productive animal is weaker against natural diseases, it will suffer a number of diseases that primitive animals did not suffer. Sometimes I think that something happens to us human beings, when civilization hunts us it improves us in a lot of things, now it also weakens us in our ability to resist. How to live without running water, without electricity, without gas? It is a tragedy, right? (Laughing)

KINTTO LUCAS. In this reality, beyond imperial consolidation, a fundamental point to analyze is the technological hegemony of the United States, which is linked to the influence of American power groups worldwide and the effects that the massification of machines can cause in human work.

Also, with a stronger Russia and China, the strengthening of the BRICS (Brazil, Russia, India, China and South Africa), it was supposed to be creating a multipolar world, in which the United States would no longer be hegemonic, but I doubt Let that be so. If we see how the United States acted to lower the price of oil, how it continues to maintain a "leadership" over Europe, how it continues to impose war to obtain economic benefits and geostrategic control - Libya and Syria are examples - we could say that despite certain ups and downs, its hegemony is still very strong.

JOSÉ MUJICA. Let's see, the truth is that the matter is quite complex, because the United States also has its serious problems, although it remains by far the military power from a technical point of view, but at a great cost too. I believe that the

United States is at the forefront, long, in the set of sciences that surround life; In the biological sciences package it has a huge advantage.

It was the first country where there was a capital nucleus of people who saw the importance of this. It is natural because the United States has always been an agricultural power, it is natural that it has studied this topic in depth because, after all, it is a country of farmers, of farmers.

These antecedents are of greater importance in the modern economy, since its research and applied computing system keep it at the forefront. If we add to this the trend in the concentration of capital, we see how it maintains its hegemony. The groups of economic power of American origin, have a formidable lobbyist influence in all the governments of the world, all of us in some way or another must suffer this scourge. And the economic concentration, plus the management of high technology, plus capital, multiplies the lobbyist influence in the entire world to gradually make a decision system in favor of these groups.

Now, again we are in the same, this does not respond to the expectation of the North American middle class, which is one more spectator, who sees how wealth is kneaded and feels victimized because it is not participating in the distribution. Thus, in that sector of society a gigantic frustration is generated that conspires against the globalization of the industrialist, concentrating, monopolistic and modernist right. So this globalization is emerging a monster that is not on the left, no! It is extreme right, it is hypernationalism and all this that we have been talking about. When Trump says he wants to address the frustration with that stagnant part of society, he takes advantage of that collective frustration of the middle class.

But all this also generates, eventually, authoritarian governments of different types, such as Turkey, such as those that may appear in Europe tomorrow, such as Putin. Each one is defending their space. I think we will attend a difficult time because of this. And to the globalizing model of transnational companies, which seemed triumphant and which was coming to a beating drum, it has all of them with it because this monster came out of which heads appear from many sides.

But there is another piece on the horizon that can shake the entire shelf: the massification of intelligent machines in human work. This is going to generate a brutal change in the work of the human being; They are going to place humanity in a collective struggle similar to the one that took place to get eight hours, or the fight for public goods.

Japan, for example, is a very technologically advanced and expensive country, surrounded by cheap labor. It has all the conditions to be a kind of vanguard in the introduction of intelligent machines at work. That technology is very useful there is no doubt. Years ago they placed a little tractor there on Mars and they could drive it from Earth for two or three years. Please !, it is not the technological problem, the technology exists, now it begins to go down to the concrete, it is produced en masse, costs are lowered, etc.

In Japan, there is already a supermarket without people, there is a company that produces 15,000 lettuces per day with machine work. 95% of the work is done by robots. This will gradually increase. There is a "miss" robot, who blinks, sings, has a 3D programmer. You play the key and it melts in the air, you understand? You can program it to sing, to move your eyes, to play it. There will come a time when they will replace humans. And what do we do there?

Changes in the way of producing change the history of humanity and the life of the worker. It is wonderful that machines replace man, because it would give a long time for humanity to live better doing other kinds of things to improve as people. But of course, the problem is that they will work for the owners of the machines, and then the contradictions of the system will be accentuated.

KINTTO LUCAS. In a world of machines, they will work for the owners, if they have any extra work ...

JOSÉ MUJICA. Sure (laughs) And the only answer will be the multiplication of public goods. Now, curiously, the second or third power in the world proposes that the work week must be shortened, do you realize? You have to work less and have the same salary, because those workers need to consume. It is the contradiction of Capitalism. The guys who think realize that if they do not distribute something, it does not sell, they do not continue creating consumers. But there is no fix, we continue in that duel.

KINTTO LUCAS. The world is experiencing a global crisis that manifests itself at the political and economic level, but is also evident in the regional and global multilateral sphere. There is an economic crisis visible in Europe, especially, and the United States. There is a crisis of world governance evidenced in the increasingly less important and less credible role of the UN (United Nations Organization), and in the oversize of a Security Council that continues to represent a historical moment that is past and past. There is a crisis of traditional multilateralism, manifested in the UN, but also in the inter-American system with a questioned OAS (Organization of American States).

The OAS, which emerged as the option of a certain historical moment in which the countries lived under the "leadership" of the United States, which was actually an imposition from that country, has almost no credibility, and if it survives it is for some interests.

There is a crisis of increasingly less credible credit multilaterals in the North and in the South, beyond some interested sectors. There is a world trade crisis evidenced in the missteps of the WTO (World Trade Organization) that finally turns to a South American to try to get out of his well; in speculation with food, and in the promotion of parasitic consumption so that the financial system survives or is strengthened by granting non-productive credits.

And within this world crisis we can also place the strengthened global and networked organized crime, increasingly linked to instances of political and economic power throughout the world. But the crisis does not touch the Empire. According to Toni Negri, today the empire assumes different forms and connotations from the traditional empire.

It is a kind of world coalition made up of countries, large corporations, the global financial system, certain multilaterals, international arbitration entities, and many other entities intertwined with each other and at the service of a global, unipolar power, which is summarized in what for Negri it is the current Empire.

The crisis does not touch the Empire in this new definition, they are the integrating processes that bring forth a diverse world opposed to the unique thought of the homogenized world politically, economically, commercially and culturally. It is the integrative processes of a new type that oppose the Empire. It is also these integrating processes that give rise to a new multilateral proposal.

Faced with the crisis of traditional multilateralism, a new multilateralism arises that is strengthened in new expressions such as BRICS (Brazil, Russia, India, China and South Africa), and in integrative processes such as those that occur in Latin America, Eurasia, Asia and Africa. Strategic processes towards a multi-polar, blocky world. But that does not end up consolidating and it seems increasingly difficult for that to happen.

In his brilliant novel The Year of the Death of Ricardo Reis, José Saramago points out "It is enough for this city to know that the compass rose exists, this is not the place where the directions open, nor is it the magnificent point where the directions converge, here precisely change directions.

Translating Saramago's words to the world system, as Immanuel Wallerstein would say, we could say that they will change directions the day we build a multipolar world system that contributes to creating a world that is a little more democratic, fairer and more equitable. In this necessary change of direction, integration is a strategic objective to achieve the independence of Latin America, but that is also long overdue. And in the duel of world capitalism, which you analyzed before, Latin

America hardly plays. What is the role of Latin America in today's world?

JOSÉ MUJICA. Latin America carries a tragedy in tow. It has the tragedy of being 10% of the world's economy, of not having a critical mass at all, of integration having failed for now. Integration is no longer just the dream of Bolívar or the great geopolitical utopia of the old liberators, it is an imperative of necessity.

We have no possibility of weighing in the balance of the world for lack of critical mass, because we cannot create a research system that gives us freedom in creativity, because we do not even have the management of certain technologies, because our universities are divorced from each other and compartmentalized from country to country, because our researchers are few ... All of this forces us to integrate.

But also, in this world, who will consider us separately? How to negotiate with China or with the countries of Europe? Are countries like Ecuador or Uruguay going to negotiate on equal terms with China? Do not be bad! We will collect, what it gives to collect at a certain juncture, but never in terms of equality, because we do not weigh. It is one thing for the Foreign Minister of Ecuador, Uruguay, etc., to each go to speak alone. Another is that one goes in the name of all of Latin America. Hey, Dad, it's different, it's another power! Our tragedy is balkanization.

On the other hand, we have in our favor a package of very valuable natural resources. We are probably the most important reserve continent in the world, but we are going to have great challenges.

The world continues to grow madly, there are those who say that Nigeria, for example, is going to have 700 million inhabitants in 40, 50 more years. I don't know what is going to happen in front of that! In any case, in this framework, integration becomes the most important chronological priority of our days.

KINTTO LUCAS. South America experienced an important moment in terms of regional integration, capitalized more clearly in Unasur, a bloc that, beyond the political or economic differences of the countries that comprise it, and certain weaknesses, managed to rise up as a space for agreements and understandings from diversity and generated a different integrating process.

Unasur, perhaps, was the most important integration proposal from South America. Those that arose before, in addition to being subregional, were conditioned by free trade, because they bet on that, not integration.

Mercosur (Common Market of the South), for example, was a proposal that emerged from free trade from neoliberalism. Although it was later processing positive changes with the emergence of progressive governments and is currently a fundamental confluence, it still has a long way to go to consolidate itself as South American Mercosur, which is the axis of a productive integration model of South Americas within Unasur. The CAN (Andean Community of Nations), on the other hand, emerged as a different integrating proposal, but finally ended up being absorbed by neoliberal hegemony in the 1990s.

For its part, Celac (Community of Latin American and Caribbean States), emerged with the need to consolidate a broad space that promotes an integrative process from Latin American plurality, from more diverse and complex processes, but without the tutelage of the United States.

Celac and Unasur arose from the Latin American and South American countries themselves and are, with all their difficulties, integration processes. The OAS was a process of imposition, not integration.

The Alba (Bolivarian Alliance for the Peoples of Our America) emerged as a proposal against the Alca (Free Trade Area of the Americas), another US imposition attempt, and has implemented complementary and solidarity processes creating interesting productive integration proposals. However, it has lacked institutional strengthening and development to achieve its consolidation.

Unasur positioned itself as a proposal for integration from a political point of view, carrying out transcendent actions to resolve conflicts, consolidate a vision of defense of common democracy, strengthen inclusive social and defense policies, and even positioning itself as a block to take into account world level in the development of a multipolar world.

It showed that, within the differences, certain agreements can be reached that start from a central point: to compete and to be heard, to be respected in a world of blocks, we have to build and participate in a compact collective from the geographical point of view. all of South America.

However, to project integration in Latin America and South America, a symbolic base must be created that supports and contributes to a culture of integration beyond the crutch of the Patria Grande. So there was no cultural change within our countries and neither was there a culture of integration

Many mistakes were made and it was necessary to go deeper into the integrating model beyond the organizations created themselves, but it was an interesting moment, perhaps one of the most interesting in the history of the ever-delayed Latin American integration. Did that possibility slip away? Did we have it close in these years?

JOSÉ MUJICA. We had it close, but we were absorbed in our national projects, in our respective concerns. This was the biggest failure of progressive governments and it is cruel to say it, but it must be said so that the generations that come from progressives have it clear, and make their mistakes but not ours, it seems to me. I would say more, for me this integration is sine qua non.

I do not think that socialism can be created within the framework of poor countries, with this I do not mean that being a rich country we are going to go to socialism, either, socialism is the son of a rich country, but they are sine qua non conditions. The other fundamental thing is integration, having a critical mass, especially in the field of research and science, which we do not have.

We are very far away, because if there is no own research, if you do not control science and technology there is no creative sovereignty for the future, you are dependent. Look what happens in the world, it turns out that Bayer is now buying from Monsanto and the Chinese are fixing with Syngenta and Doptone. So what is going to happen? There will be three economic groups that produce the seeds of the world, with all that that means for the agriculture of the world ...

KINTTO LUCAS. Whoever controls the seeds, in some way will control the food of the world. Where will food sovereignty be?

JOSÉ MUJICA. All the farmers in the world are going to be mediators of these companies, because we are going to work for them. How to deal with that? Do you realize what it means? Can one speak of sovereignty without knowledge ownership? No! So, for me, integration is a chronological priority, and because it is a chronological priority, it forces us politically.

We would have to throw the famous democratic clause in the street, because that is a good clause so that, take that straw away from me, we are divided. If integration is a great cause, it has to condition everything else. And if there is a dictatorship, I will quietly bank on it as long as I am not torpedoed by integration. I am putting an extreme case, and I say that I have to bank it because if I do not do it, in the name of democracy the already built integration can be dismembered. Also, if I'm going to wait for all Latin Americans to be socialists to integrate, goodbye.

I have a socializing vision, I cannot give it up, but what socialism can we speak of from an isolated country in Latin America? We are crazy! This discussion already existed in the time of Trotsky and Stalin, right? In today's world, worse! To say that we are going to make a socialist country, don't screw around!

KINTTO LUCAS. Precisely, and we are not lying
to people when we tell them that we are creating
the socialism of the 21st century and invent a
whole story to justify it theoretically? Or do we
invent the socialism of good living and other
stories?

JOSÉ MUJICA. Sure, they are chimeras we sow.
We are mending, trying to mend and make less
aggressive this Capitalism in which we live. We
aim as much as possible to develop a certain germ
of socialism, but from there ... nothing more. And
we cannot count people ... As I said before: critical
mass as a whole is decisive for me, because if we
achieve a common space, things change, things
start to change, because there we do have another
stature in the world . And to consider socialism, it
is sine qua non to have a critical mass.

KINTTO LUCAS. But there are some foundations
that we can build without saying that we are going
to socialism. There are some fundamental points

that need to be deepened and can be deepened. The consolidation of a citizen democracy in the sociopolitical are not a chimera; an agrarian revolution that has effects on the social and the productive and is linked to consolidating food sovereignty; the construction of greater citizen participation from a political-organizational perspective; and the strengthening of the social and solidarity economy economically.

For me, socialism will always be socialism, beyond the fact that it must be adapted to the concrete reality of each historical moment.

I remember that in 1992, before the 500th anniversary of the conquest, I wrote a short essay on Latin American socialism and its peculiarities. What is called in Ecuador or Bolivia Buen Vivir or Sumak Kawsay is not synonymous with socialism, but it is an important point in the construction of a path of national liberation.

It is a way of incorporating some particularities of Latin America into a socialist thought, from a mestizo thought. The mistake is to make people believe that you are already in socialism, or that you made a revolution, when you did not even do anything to process a cultural change and create, at least, citizens ...

In this sense, there is an issue that is also a priority, but it is contradictory, such as the environment. You have vindicated the issue in different forums but in particular in the Eco 20 years, with a speech that had a great impact. But how to overcome the contradiction that has arisen between the need to save the environment that some say and the need to extract natural resources to overcome the poverty that others claim?

JOSÉ MUJICA. The appalling need to extract natural resources is the daughter of functional consumerist culture to Capitalism. We have created a civilization of waste, which is based on inventing a number of devices and issues, which also have to be short-lived, because you have to throw them away quickly so that other things come to replace them ...

The accumulation of garbage is becoming a problem Endemic throughout the world, the expression of this is the other side of the defense of the environment ... The first defense of the environment is human culture, if we are attacking nature with this waste of energy and means, the environment is doomed.

So everything depends on human culture, if we are going to tolerate Capitalism doing these things, we have replaced the religious God with the market God, who is the one who organizes our life, so let's say we are ecologists.

Ecology, as a philosophy in itself, if it is not imbued with the human political drama, is like the dreamer who wants to humanize Capitalism. That guy can't stand humanization, because Capitalism is made to generate profits, surplus value. It is that, you cannot solve it, there is no way to humanize it, you will not change it. The greatest ecologists change cars, they cannot give up many things, they consume and consume ... So we are in the same.

KINTTO LUCAS. (Laughter) And there are the cities ... increasingly unlivable ... You must remember a tango by Astor Piazzola and Amelita Baltar, in which they asked themselves, many years ago, why the cities? But the city became the central axis of life in many countries. It ceased to be a place and became a character that, sometimes can devour and other times forget the people who pass through it. The current city is home to nomadic beings, inhabitants of the world rather than of the neighborhood. Tenants of life who walk through it with uncertainty in tow and loneliness. Human types who question their belonging to a place but adapt to the trip.

All cities belong to them and yet none belongs to them. They are the eternal travelers of a time marked by uprooting. For the friendship via facebook, the reality lived on twitter, the memory recovered in selfie, instagram or any of those social networks that may also be antisocial. Globalization put all cities within reach and yet removed them from sensitivity, dehumanized them. The city becomes the precise stage for representation. We are all characters in a great plot.

The fleeting, momentary selfie can be irrefutable proof of having passed by somewhere and at the same time another irony of the city, since it often only represents reality. It is not deception, it is just the adjustment of reality. The selfie is a form of ephemeral power. Sometimes a faithful document and sometimes it can no longer replace the city but the subject that transits it.

The selfie is also a way of seeing. Reality is built through what everyone sees. The inhabitants of the city live based on images created by their gaze. Those images are like metaphors of the relationship with their neighbors and their environment. The confluence of reality-image-imagination-hyperreality are an essential part of today's city. But that current city has its opponent in the city of memory, the one that refuses to disappear. Then there can be a contrast, often tense with the past, when the city of memory rescues social or personal history to confront it with oblivion.

JOSÉ MUJICA. That is cruel, it has no mercy. But it is a fact, look, look (pointing out to the buildings) we have people piled up in the city, we invented this ...

Then we have to spend energy in heaps for everything to work. Since it does not give us life to withstand traffic, we have to drill the earth to the bottom (laughs). Imagine! You have to drill more and more to make transport routes. Smaller cities are more humane, you can go to work by bike or on foot, no matter if you are nearby.

They are more colloquial cities and one can be on a quiet sidewalk, or use the train and other types of transportation, but with a certain human measure. Civilization made the leap from small towns. The Hellenic civilization grew up in small cities. When the city grew a lot, they founded a colony or another city.

These megalopolises that we are making are Cement Jungles, incubators of loneliness, because they are made by real estate, by business, to obtain surplus value, not for human happiness. And therein lies the paradox, there are thousands of houses without people and thousands of people without homes ... We have to rethink everything, because we have the instruments for that, we have the instruments to change that reality ...

KINTTO LUCAS. That does not lead us to the issue of Social Networks, which are there and that people live from, and finally it seems that friends have them on social networks, not in the neighborhood. There are also fewer and fewer neighborhoods like those in which we grew up, in which there was a friendly, almost communal relationship. How can you build a closer world with that reality?

JOSÉ MUJICA. In the old Greek civilization nothing was said too much, so what is a formidable

instrument becomes an addiction and slavery.
People are enslaved, if we start looking at the
street, there are the couples in a bowling alley,
young men, who instead of pampering each other,
holding hands, kissing, are looking at a little
screen, right? It's crazy ...

Sometimes I think if the human being has reached
the top of what he can, because we need to stop
reasoning as countries, even as a continent, to start
reasoning much more as a species ... Globalizations
there were several in history, for example, the
Empire Chino was a globalization in its time, Rome
was a brutal globalization, you have to see how
long it lasted, but there was always a political
epicenter, a command. He had a lot of military
boots, unquestionable, because all globalizations
were made at a redoubled pace, but with political
leadership.

This globalization is more intense than any other
because it is spreading a more or less similar way
of living on the entire planet, with certain similar
average values, but it does not have a political
command, the command is diffuse, it is the market
itself, it is like a civilization that goes and works
without intelligence ... I never saw such a thing ...

This is like an anonymous intention that governs us, because in reality globalization governs us, we do not govern it, we suffer from it. So I ask myself this question: have we reached the limits of what a human being can give? The human being as a political capacity for self-government. I don't know, I don't have an answer and I'm distressed, but we have to start asking these questions.

On the other hand, contemporary political discourse is passionate, and if you are looking for any idea that makes you think of Europe's discourse, you will not have any luck. I was cold when I heard Hollande's speech, because one has inside that mythology of the French Revolution, which I know, pure nonsense. German social democracy disappeared. He disappeared!

So, I don't know, you can hardly see a glow in "Podemos" (referring to "Unidas Podemos"), a different thought that appears in that Spain, but almost nothing. In the United States, I'm not going to tell you, Obama is a left-wing radical next to what is coming, including Mrs. Clinton.

It is interesting that a candidate appeared who had a very interesting university following, like Sanders, because the best of the United States is in the Universities. There you will find a world that fills you with joy and hope and the same thing happens in other universities in the world.

The best of England is in Cambridge, at least there are people who think! I have also seen it in Turkey, in Japan, there is a university youth who is not in conformity with the world in which they live, although they do not know where they are going to grab, but they are not divorced from the world they have to live in, and that does give a bit of hope.

I mean, I want to convey a complex feeling. We in Uruguay met a proletariat in which we bet a lot of hope and sleep, dressed in brin, used to wear a leather or rough cap, had a huge manly look, sometimes, at a redoubled pace, came on October 8 or other avenues.

Now, it seems to me that the most revolutionary class that is coming is going to be in a robe, is entering the universities, they are going to be qualified workers in tertiary education, not for human reasons, but that the system itself due to technological advance is what is going to require. That will be the worker who will leave more surplus value, but it will be much more difficult to lower, more difficult for them to handle. Perhaps its weakness is that it will be much more modern.

KINTTO LUCAS. Reencountering old Pepe on the path of life always brings emotions and memories, and of course, more than an interview it was a conversation between two colleagues. But before finishing, it is impossible not to mention one of the most important political and social leaders in the history of Uruguay, who had a Latin American significance, despite the historical moment he had to live through: Raúl Sendic, an advanced thinker of his time , founder of the tupamaros, someone about whom we could not stop talking, and also recounts the strength of those Quixotes who joined the tupamara guerrillas ...

JOSÉ MUJICA. Sendic was an intellectual countryman, very rare, the strangest thing. Conqueror of people around the stove, of small crowds, but crowds at the end, and committed to the dream of social transformations, but very down-to-earth, especially in the most advanced stage of his life. Heterodox by nature, defender of Rosa Luxemburg in the field of thought, incredible forecaster of the fall of the Soviet Union, of what was called the socialist bloc, I do not know how he had detected symptoms of the disease that others had not detected. And that it contributed to make up part of our heritage between socialist and libertarian, those of us who were lucky to have known him, to have walked with him.

Most likely, his most important contribution to those who knew him, to those who walked with him, was to be a friend of anti-schema freedom of thought, that defiant freedom of, in the right or in the mistake, thinking with your own head. Is one thing that many of us owe it to him. And well, it was an anti-figure figure.

KINTTO LUCAS. After reviewing so many people who were left on the road, so many struggles, a question arises in the midst of memories and conversation. Have you ever wondered if the fight started by you was worth it?

JOSÉ MUJICA. Yes, of course ... We are children of circumstances, of a moment in world history, also in Latin America. Our dream was to change society and the essence of capitalist society, to be able to reach a change of power, to effect transformations through the constitution of a new building of citizenship. Of course, we could not see the difficulties, we are grandchildren of extreme rationalism and we had a package of conviction, which was naive in the face of the complexities of history. We have made some progress, we are not clear about what to do, but we are clear about what not to do ...

KINTTO LUCAS. But it's quite ...

JOSÉ MUJICA. It is enough, we are not on record zero. Now from an individual point of view, I think that at that time we lived the best stage of our life, because we went to the fight fifty, with an altruism that today must seem quixotic and fictional. We left everything on the road: family, passing, security, we put the leather on the line, we mortgaged the years of our youth, which were gone ...

It was a moment of wonderful explosion of the inner strength of people who believe in something and establish how much the human being is capable of when they believe in something ... What strength we had! What strength! We long for it of course and above all we long for not being able to pass it on to the new generations. We live it in a moment, in a spark of history, in today's world it is unthinkable. So much Don Quixote, so much poetry, is unthinkable ...

———————————————

(1) Old Andrés Cultelli, a recognized socialist activist who joined the MLN-T in the 1960s. He died a few years ago.

KINTTO LUCAS.

Uruguayan-Ecuadorian writer and journalist.
Master in Advanced Studies in Spanish and Latin
American Literature from the University of
Barcelona. Latin American Journalism Award José
Martí 1990. Vice Chancellor of Ecuador, 2010-
2012. Itinerant Ambassador of Uruguay for
UNASUR, CELAC, ALBA and Integration, 2013.
Pen of Dignity of the National Union of Journalists
of Ecuador 2004.

He was a professor of journalism and political and
geopolitical news and lecturer at various
universities, state institutions and international
organizations. Advisor to the Constituent Assembly
of Ecuador, 2008.

He was director and editor of various newspapers
and magazines, correspondent for the Inter Press
Service Agency and has written for various Latin
American and European media. He received the
Grand Cross Degree Merit Decoration from the

Government of Peru and the Ho Chi Minh Gold Button from Vietnam.

Some of his books are: *Indigenous and Black Rebellions in Latin America*; *Women of the 20th century*; *The Indian Rebellion* (in English with the title *We Will Not Dance on Our Grandparent's Tombs. Indigenous uprisings in Ecuador*); *Plan Colombia. Armed peace*; *The indigenous movement and the acrobatics of the colonel*; *Flavored with a goal -football and journalism-*; *Rafael Correa: A stranger in Carondelet*; *The war at home –From Reyes to the Manta Base-*; *As is - José Mujica's path to the presidency*; *The Ark of Reality –from the culture of silence to wikileaks-*; *Written Portraits*; *Ecuador Cara y Cruz: from the uprising of the nineties to the Citizen Revolution* (Three Volumes); *Enrique Lucas and a question for Pessoa*; *Scheherazade and other stories*; *The Shipwreck of Humanity*; *Facts and Fictions: About books, writers and readers*; *Mercé Rodoreda, Barcelona and the "I-City"* and *Como en Aquelarre*. It has an unpublished novel that will appear before the end of 2020, an unpublished book of short stories and a novel to finish.